Laugh Out Loud Canadian Jokes

Scholastic Canada Ltd.
604 King Street West, Toronto, Ontario M5V 1E1, Canada

Scholastic Inc.
557 Broadway, New York, NY 10012, USA

Scholastic Australia Pty Limited
PO Box 579, Gosford, NSW 2250, Australia

Scholastic New Zealand Limited
Private Bag 94407, Botany, Manukau 2163, New Zealand

Scholastic Children's Books
Euston House, 24 Eversholt Street, London NW1 1DB, UK

www.scholastic.ca

Library and Archives Canada Cataloguing in Publication
Laugh out loud Canadian jokes / cover illustration by Bill Dickson ;
interior illustrations by Bill Dickson and Dominique Pelletier.
"Previously published as 101 Canadian Jokes by Howard Hershkowitz,
101 Cool Canadian Jokes by Erin O'Connor, 101 Creepy Canadian
Jokes by Stella Partheniou Grasso and 101 Hockey Jokes by Kara
Woodburn. With additional material from 101 Best Jokes Ever, 101
Math Jokes by Erin O'Connor and Chrissy Bozik and Great Canadian
Puzzles by Audrey and Dodie McKim and Edith Fowke."

ISBN 978-1-4431-2886-5 (softcover)

1. Canadian wit and humor (English)--Juvenile literature. 2. Canadian
wit and humor, Pictorial--Juvenile literature. I. Dickson, Bill, illustrator
I. Pelletier, Dominique, 1975-, illustrator III. Title: Canadian jokes.

PN6231.C19L39 2017   j818'.602   C2017-900227-9

Photos ©: cover star: Logorilla/iStockphoto.
Interior illustrations by Bill Dickson and Dominique Pelletier.
Material from *101 Canadian Jokes* copyright © 2004 by Scholastic Canada Ltd.
Material from *101 Cool Canadian Jokes* copyright © 2005 by Erin O'Connor.
Material from *101 Creepy Canadian Jokes* copyright © 2011 by Stella Partheniou Grasso.
Material from *101 Hockey Jokes* copyright © 2012 by Kara Woodburn.
Material from *101 Best Jokes Ever* copyright © 2004 by Scholastic Canada Ltd.
Material from *101 Math Jokes* copyright © 2011 by Erin O'Connor and Chrissy Bozik.
Material from *Great Canadian Puzzles* copyright © 1974 by Audrey McKim and Dorothy McKim;
copyright © 1982 by Edith Fowke.
All other text copyright © 2017 by Scholastic Canada Ltd.
Illustrations copyright © 2004, 2005, 2007, 2011, 2012, 2017 by Scholastic Canada Ltd.

10 9 8 7 6   Printed in Canada 114   21 22 23 24 25

Laugh Out Loud Canadian Jokes

Previously published as *101 Canadian Jokes* by Howard Hershkowitz, *101 Cool Canadian Jokes* by Erin O'Connor, *101 Creepy Canadian Jokes* by Stella Partheniou Grasso and *101 Hockey Jokes* by Kara Woodburn.

With additional material from *101 Best Jokes Ever, 101 Math Jokes* by Erin O'Connor and Chrissy Bozik and *Great Canadian Puzzles* by Audrey and Dodie McKim and Edith Fowke.

Cover illustration by Bill Dickson

Scholastic Canada Ltd.

Toronto New York London Auckland Sydney
Mexico City New Delhi Hong Kong Buenos Aires

Oh Canada!

What did the Canadian flag say
to the pole?

Nothing, it just waved.

Did you hear the one about the cottager who lit a fire in her boat and had to swim ashore when it sank?

It just goes to show, you can't have your kayak and heat it too!

What did the man say when his neighbour finished building his igloo?

"That's an ice house you have there!"

If you're Canadian in the kitchen, what are you in the bathroom?

European.

What does Canada produce that no other country produces?

Canadians.

George: *Come on, Sam, hurry up!*
Sam: *I'm rushin', I'm rushin'!*
George: *That's funny, I thought you were Canadian!*

Why did the rancher ride his horse?

Because the horse was too heavy to carry.

What did the paddle say when the oar called?

Canoe speak up? I can't hear you!

Why didn't anyone ask the maple tree to the dance?

Because it wasn't poplar.

How does a Timbit get around
in winter?

On doughshoes.

What do negative Canadians
drive?

Ski-Don'ts!

If a plane crashes on the US/Canada border, where does the law require the survivors to be buried?

Nowhere, silly — you don't bury the survivors!

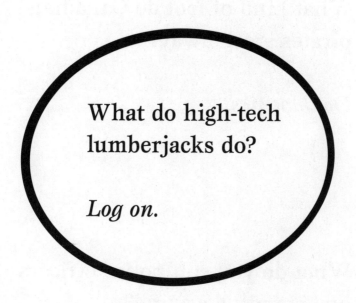

What do high-tech
lumberjacks do?

Log on.

What kind of loot do Canadian pirates stash away?

Doubloonies.

What do you call police officers just standing around?

The Royal Canadian Dismounted Police.

How does a Mountie stay in
the saddle?

With maple stirrups.

What is the logger's favourite
nursery rhyme?

Lumberjack and Jill.

Where did the clumsy voyageur go?

On a canoe trip.

What's yellow, has red hair and freckles, and lives in PEI?

Banana of Green Gables!

19

Top 10 Canadian Bestsellers:

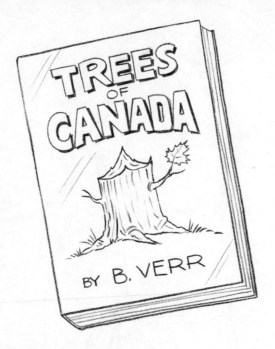

1. *Beavers: Friend or Foe?*
   by May Poll

2. *Canada: The Greatest Country
   in the World*
   by Ken Nuck

3. *The Wonderful World of Doughnuts*
   by I.M. Dieting

4. *Everything You Need to Know about Moss and Lichen*
   by Carrie Boo

5. *Designing Snow Houses*
   by Iggy Lou

6. *Once Upon a Waterway*
   by Laurence Seaway

7. *The Night the Furnace Broke*
   by R.U. Chilly

8. *The Stampede Encyclopedia*
   by Al Berta

9. *The Missing Mitten Mystery*
   by I.C. Fingers

10. *Trees of Canada*
    by B. Verr

How do ghosts take their coffee?

Double-double: two boogers, *two screams.*

Who's the king of the skeletons' Winter Carnival?

Bone Homme.

Why do ghosts like dimes and quarters?

One has the Boonose schooner, the other has a cariboo.

What airline do ghouls fly with?

Scare Canada.

Why did the hockey player open a Tim Hortons?

He was a franchise player!

How did vampires come to Canada?

On blood vessels.

What is another term for a hockey fan?

Canadian!

What time is it when the quarter chases the loonie?

Quarter after one!

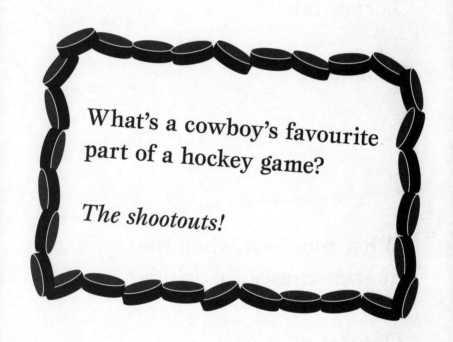

What's a cowboy's favourite part of a hockey game?

The shootouts!

What do they call James Bond
in Newfoundland?

007:30.

What do you call a Canadian
T. Rex?

Dino-sorry.

How is the moon like a loonie?

It has four quarters.

What occurs early in Canada
but late in Quebec?

The letter C.

What do you get when you cross
a lake with a leaky boat?

About halfway, if you're lucky!

What do you call a rich baker?

*A dough*nut!

Riddle, Riddle!

1. When is a train like water?
2. When are men and women of the RCMP like oranges?
3. What is the strongest bird in Canada?
4. When is our weather like a king?
5. What Canadian cup has no handles?
6. Every child in Canada spends much time making it, yet no one can see it. What is it?
7. How do you know Peace River is rich?
8. Why do people swim in Lake Ontario?

Answers on page 380.

Hey, Mom! There's a Canadian at the Door!

Knock, knock!
Who's there?
Canoe.
Canoe who?
Canoe tell me some knock-knock jokes?

Knock, knock!
Who's there?
Toboggan.
Toboggan who?
I like toboggan with salespeople.

Knock, knock!
Who's there?
Gander.
Gander who?
*I be-gander worry you
wouldn't ask!*

Knock, knock!
Who's there?
Terrace.
Terrace who?
Terrace no place like BC!

Knock, knock!
Who's there?
Amos.
Amos who?
Amosquito just bit me.

Knock, knock!
Who's there?
Andy.
Andy who?
Andy just bit me again!

Knock, knock!
Who's there?
Snow.
Snow who?
Snowbody but me!

Knock, knock!
Who's there?
Water.
Water who?
Water you doing? We're late for the game!

Knock, knock!
Who's there?
Icy.
Icy who?
Icy you're not expecting me!

Knock, knock!
Who's there?
Tuque.
Tuque who?
Tuque you by surprise,
didn't I?

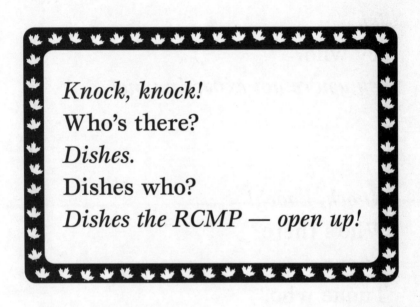

Knock, knock!
Who's there?
Dishes.
Dishes who?
Dishes the RCMP — open up!

Knock, knock!
Who's there?
Snow.
Snow who?
Snow fun standing out here in the cold!

Knock, knock!
Who's there?
Yukon.
Yukon who?
Yukon let me in now!

Knock, knock!
Who's there?
Icing!
Icing who?
*Icing "O Canada" before
the game!*

Knock, knock!
Who's there?
Wheat.
Wheat who?
*Wheat a minute — I've got
the wrong house!*

Knock, knock!
Who's there?
Caribou!
Caribou who?
Don't cry — it's only a joke!

Knock, knock!
Who's there?
Winna.
Winna who?
*Winna-peg, but I want to
win a Stanley Cup!*

Knock, knock!
Who's there?
Gordie.
Gordie who?
*Gordie Howe do you not
know who I am?*

Trick or Treat!

Trick or treat!
Who's there?
Ivana.
Ivana who?
Ivana candy, please.

Trick or treat!
Who's there?
Slime.
Slime who?
Slime freezing out here.
Let me in!

48

Trick or treat!
Who's there?
Bat.
Bat who?
*Batter give me my treat before
I give you my trick.*

Trick or treat!
Who's there?
Ooze.
Ooze who?
Ooze in there and why are you hoarding all the candy?

Trick or treat!
Who's there?
Owl.
Owl who?
Owl stop knocking if you stop hooting.

Trick or treat!
Who's there?
Witch.
Witch who?
Witching I had a treat
right now.

Trick or treat!
Who's there?
Fright.
Fright who?
Fright now I'd do anything for a candy.

Trick or treat!
Who's there?
Boo.
Boo who?
Why are you crying?
I'm the one the ghost is after.

Hockey Hilarity

What do a hockey player and a magician have in common?

Both do hat tricks!

What do you get when you cross a groundhog with a Maple Leaf?

Six more weeks of hockey.

What goes all around a hockey rink but never moves?

The boards.

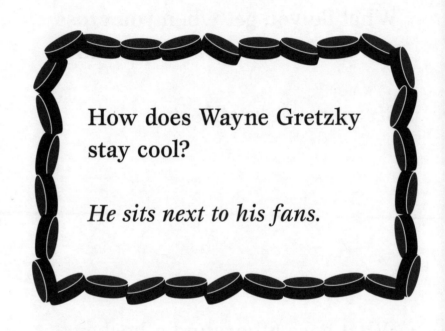

How does Wayne Gretzky
stay cool?

He sits next to his fans.

What sport do bare feet like
to play?

Ice sockey.

What sport do cats like to play?

Mice hockey.

What lives in water and plays hockey?

A skate fish.

What sport do squares like to play?

Ice blockey.

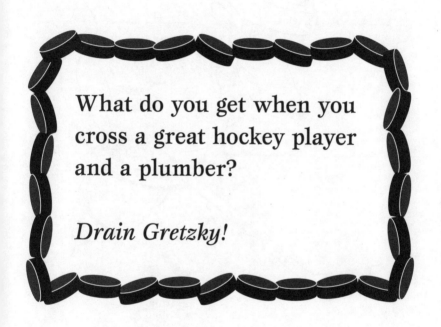

What do you get when you cross a great hockey player and a plumber?

Drain Gretzky!

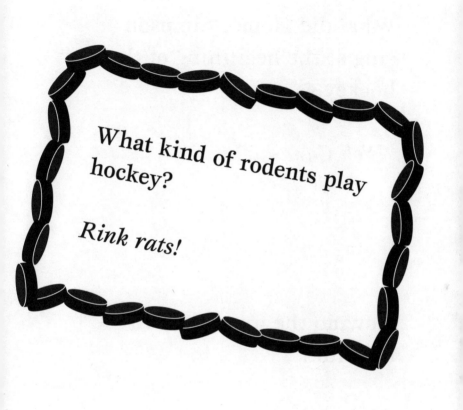

What kind of rodents play hockey?

Rink rats!

What did Homer Simpson sing at the beginning of the hockey game?

"D'oh Canada."

How do the undead clean the rink?

With a Zombonie.

Why was the hockey player's cake so plain?

He forgot the icing!

Why was there a delay at airport security?

All the hockey players were getting checked!

What's a ghost's favourite show?

Hockey Fright in Canada with Don Scary.

70

Who is the most important player on the ghosts' hockey team?

The ghoulie.

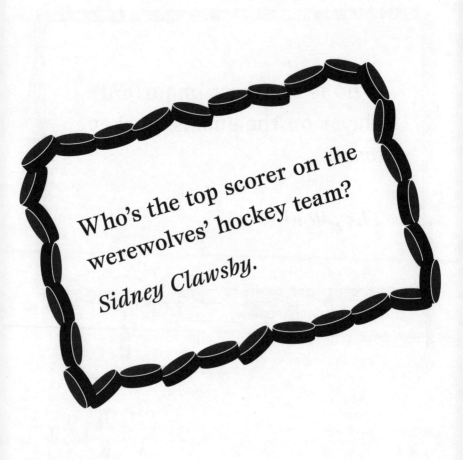

Who's the top scorer on the werewolves' hockey team?

Sidney Clawsby.

What does a hockey player do on vacation?

He takes a break*away!*

What hot beverage do enforcers drink?

Penaltea!

Why was the hockey player cold all the time?

He was number one in the draft!

Why was the goalie late for practice?

She was having dinner with friends at the crossbar!

What does a winning
team drink at breakfast?

A *Stanley Cup* of coffee!

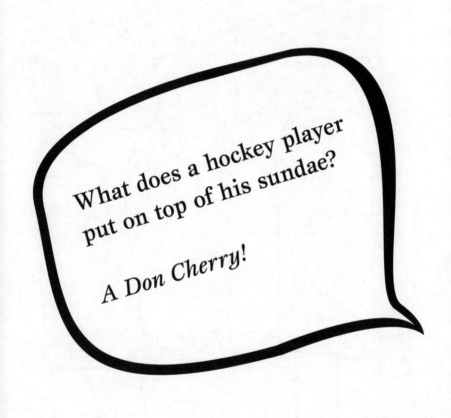

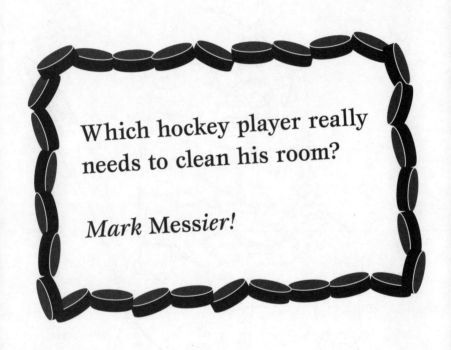

Which hockey player really
needs to clean his room?

Mark Messier!

Where did the goalie like
to shop?

Any place he could save!

What do you call a hockey player
lying on his back or front?

*Off*side!

What do you call a hockey player when he's lying on his stomach?

Back*up!*

Why did the hockey player take up javelin throwing?

He liked high-sticking!

Why did the offensive coach get frustrated when he checked his email?

He had too many forwards!

Why did the goalie on a losing streak have such long arms?

The coach kept pulling him!

Why did the police officer think the right winger was a thief?

He had possession of the puck!

Why did the hockey player limp when he walked?

He had a toe drag.

Why couldn't fans recognize the star forward?

He had his faceoff!

What do you call a hockey player who loses his house keys?

A shutout!

Why did the hockey player go to court?

To plead to the goal judge!

How does a hockey player watch a movie at home?

She presses power play!

Why was the hockey player not "It" when he was tagged?

He was in the neutral zone!

What is a hockey player's favourite dairy product?

Top cheese!

Why were the parents banned from the game?

They were smothering the puck!

What is a hockey player's least favourite dessert?

A turnover!

Capital Humour

How do you make the prime minister fly?

Put him on a plane.

Where do pickles have their government buildings?

On Parliament Dill!

What do you get when you cross the prime minister with a battery?

Someone who's really in charge!

What do you call a hockey
player who serves in the army?

Major Penalty!

What do you get when you cross
the prime minister with an owl?

Someone who gives a hoot!

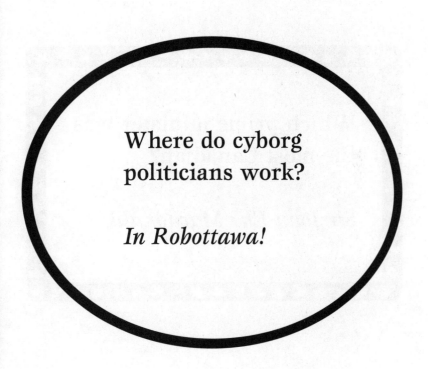

Where do cyborg
politicians work?

In Robottawa!

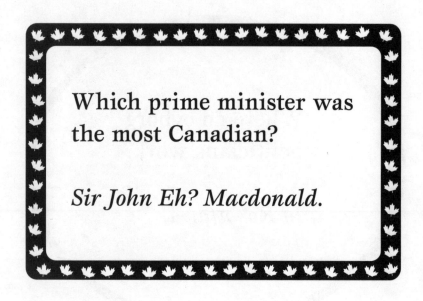

Which prime minister was the most Canadian?

Sir John Eh? Macdonald.

99

100

What's smelly, green and gross, and works on Parliament Hill?

The slime minister!

What's the capital of Creepy Canada?

Rottawa.

Why did the swamp monster win the election?

Voters wanted a green candidate.

How can a poltergeist serve his country?

He can join the Ghost Guard.

How did the werewolf become prime minister?

He clawed his way to the top.

Why will the abominable snowman never try to eat the Peace Tower again?

It was too time-consuming.

Wild Canada!

Why do seagulls live near the sea?

If they lived near the bay, they'd be bagels.

What is big and white and
found in Vancouver?

A lost polar bear.

What has one hump, is brown
and wanders Nunavut?

A lost camel.

How do you get milk from a polar bear?

Raid its fridge and run like mad.

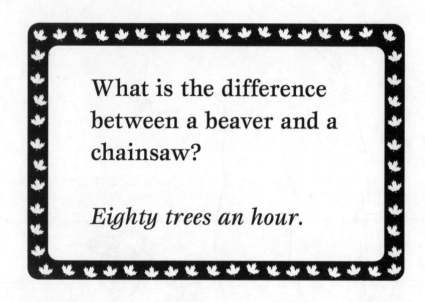

What is the difference between a beaver and a chainsaw?

Eighty trees an hour.

How do you keep a grizzly bear from charging?

Take away its credit cards.

What do you call a polar bear with no socks on?

Bearfoot.

What did the Canada goose
say when she saw a plate of
scrambled eggs?

*"What a bunch of mixed-up
kids!"*

Who does a dog quarterback
throw to?

A Labrador receiver.

What do you call a dog
that sits in a snowdrift?

A *chili dog!*

Where does a 300-kilo grizzly bear sit?

Anywhere it wants.

What kind of pine has the sharpest needles?

The porcupine.

What did the beaver say to the maple tree?

"It's been nice gnawing you."

What do you call a herd of giggling cattle?

*Laughing*stock.

Where do sled drivers keep dog food?

In the mush*room.*

How do you catch
a squirrel?

Climb a tree and act
like a nut!

Why did the rancher take his cow to the vet?

Because she was moooody.

What is the Canada goose's favourite TV show?

The feather report.

What bird gasps and pants on Newfoundland's coast?

A puff*in.*

What kind of bears like to go out in the rain?

Drizzly bears.

Why do polar bears wear fur coats?

Because they would look silly in ski jackets.

What should you do when you're surrounded by polar bears, cougars and killer whales?

Hope you're at the zoo!

What airline do grizzlies fly?

Bear Canada.

Where do husky dogs live?

In the Barktic!

What did the maple tree say to the woodpecker?

Leaf me alone!

Where do farmers in the north keep their hogs?

In pigloos!

What do frogs like to play?

Toad hockey.

Why does Santa Claus use reindeer to pull his sleigh?

Because moose can't fly.

Why did the chicken show up
for training camp?

He thought he made the rooster.

Why can't the T. Rex hockey
team win any games?

*Because they're always short-
handed.*

What are the scariest animals?

Cariboos!

What do you get when you cross
a lobster with a supermodel?

A snappy dresser!

Oh, You Canucklehead!

What do you call a foolish Canadian?

A Canucklehead!

Canucklehead: *Doctor, I feel like a jelly doughnut!*
Doctor: *What's gotten into you?*
Canucklehead: *Flour, sugar and raspberry filling.*

Canucklehead: *Doctor, people are saying I'm weird because I love doughnuts.*
Doctor: *That's nonsense. Lots of people love doughnuts.*
Canucklehead: *What a relief! Do you want to come to the wedding?*

Teacher: *Why is there a maple leaf on our flag?*
Canucklehead: *Because the whole tree wouldn't fit!*

Canucklehead: *Doctor, I swallowed a dollar!*
Doctor: *How do you feel?*
Canucklehead: *Loonie!*

Canucklehead: *Doctor, my eye hurts every time I drink hot chocolate!*
Doctor: *Then take the spoon out of the cup first!*

Why did the Canucklehead bury his wallet in the snow?

He wanted cold, hard cash.

Canucklehead: *Doctor, I feel awful. What's wrong with me?*
Doctor: *You've got doughnuts up your nose, poutine in your ears and maple syrup on your head. I don't think you're eating right.*

Canucklehead: *Doctor, I swallowed a whole doughnut.*
Doctor: *Are you choking?*
Canucklehead: *No, I'm completely serious!*

Teacher: *Why are you wearing flippers to school?*
Canucklehead: *To keep grizzly bears away.*
Teacher: *But there aren't any grizzly bears around here.*
Canucklehead: *See — it works!*

Canucklehead: Doctor, I think I'm a Labrador retriever.

Doctor: How long have you felt this way?

Canucklehead: Since I was a puppy!

141

What kind of underwear
does a Canucklehead wear?

Maple briefs.

Why did the Canucklehead move up north to Tuktoyaktuk?

Because he wanted to be cool!

Why did the Canucklehead cross the road?

To prove he wasn't chicken.

Why did the Canucklehead stop
ice fishing?

The Zamboni was coming.

How do you keep a Canucklehead
in suspense?

I'll tell you tomorrow!

What happened to the Canucklehead who thought he was a Canada goose?

He flew south for the winter!

DR. FRANKENSTEIN, DR. FRANKENSTEIN!

Patient: *Doctor, I'm having trouble sleeping.*

Dr. Frankenstein: *I can tell. You look dead tired.*

Patient: *Doctor, I think I'm a skeleton.*
Dr. Frankenstein: *Don't be such a bonehead.*

Patient: *Doctor, I'm having trouble smelling.*
Dr. Frankenstein: *That's utter nonscents.*

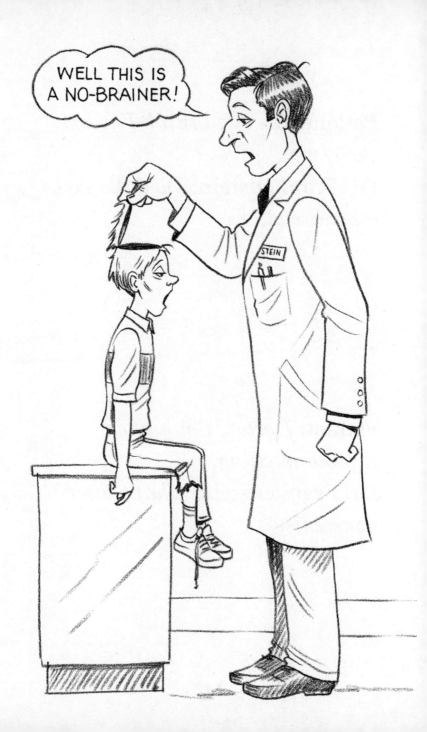

Patient: Doctor, I think I'm a zombie.

Dr. Frankenstein: Well this is a no-brainer.

Patient: *Doctor, I think I'm a vampire.*
Dr. Frankenstein: *You're just a little batty, is all.*

Patient: *Doctor, my nightmares are out of control.*
Dr. Frankenstein: *Hold your horses.*

From Sea to Silly Sea

If a man was born in France, then raised in England, moved to Canada and died in Quebec, what is he?

Dead.

Did you hear about the guy who just flew in from St. John's?

Boy, were his arms tired!

If a toonie and a loonie were on the Calgary Tower, which would jump off first?

The loonie, because it has less cents.

Where do polar bears vote?

The North Poll.

What's in the middle of Alberta?

The letter E.

Sean: *Where were you born?*
Greg: *Nova Scotia.*
Sean: *What part?*
Greg: *All of me!*

What do you get when you put a chicken on top of the CN Tower?

Beacon and eggs.

159

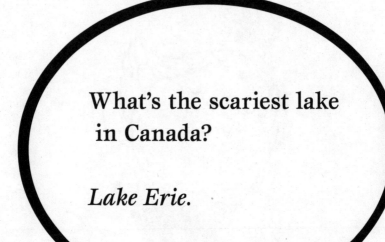

What's the scariest lake
in Canada?

Lake Erie.

What's the best lake in Canada?

Lake Superior.

Jane: *So, have you lived in British Columbia all your life?*
Sue: *Not yet.*

Canadian Riddles

1. Why can't a man living in Halifax be buried west of the Red River?

2. What Canadian animals are found in banks?

3. How far can a dog run into the northern woods?

4. Is it legal for a man in Saskatchewan to marry his widow's sister?

5. A Canadian builds a house rectangular in shape. Each side has a southern exposure. A big bear comes wandering by the house. What colour is the bear?

Answers on page 380.

What is the Yukoner's favourite song?

Freeze a jolly good fellow.

What is the lake monster's favourite toy?

An Ogopogo stick.

Where does the tallest man
in the world get clean?

The CN Shower.

What's huge, green and found
in Sudbury, Ontario?

The Big Pickle!

What is bread made with
in Nunavut?

Iqaluwheat.

What mountains like to fight?

The Rocky Mountains!

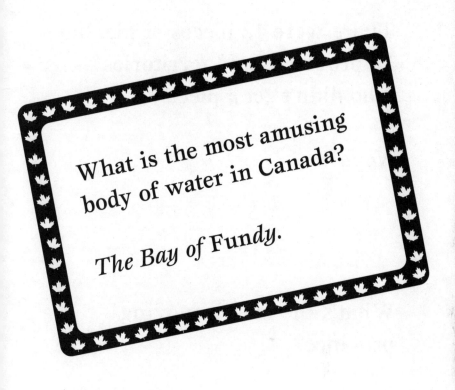

What is the most amusing body of water in Canada?

The Bay of Fundy.

There were 12 pieces of pie, but 13 provinces and territories — who didn't get a piece?

Nunavut.

What's the most annoying province?

Pinch Edward Island.

Where does the river always trip?

Niagara Falls!

Why did the envelope go to Calgary?

For the Stamp*ede.*

Where is the scariest place in Canada?

The Yukon Terrortory.

Why?

Because Yukon't hide from the abominable snowman.

Which province is frightening?

Onscareio!

What caped crusader helps those in need across the Prairies?

Flatman!

Why is the Bay of Fundy so clean?

Because of the Tide.

What is the wimpiest landmark in Canada?

The CN Cower.

Where did the zombie go on vacation?

Deadmonton.

What's the scariest astronomical phenomenon?

The Northern Frights.

What do zombies farm in PEI?

Finger*ling potatoes.*

Why did the wraith hide in the fog off the coast of St. John's?

It wanted to be mist.

Why did the ghost go to the Calgary Stampede?

*To see the night*mares.

Why did the Grim Reaper visit Sudbury?

To see the Big Sickle.

Where did Ogopogo go on vacation?

Lake Eerie.

Where does Bigfoot live?

Sasquatchewan.

Why did the zombie go to Canada's Wonderland?

Because it has great roller ghosters.

What kind of spider lives in the CN Tower?

The Torontula.

Why wasn't the ogre
allowed on the
Confederation Bridge?

He refused to pay the
troll fees.

Attention Sports Fans

What sort of ball doesn't bounce?

A snowball.

How do you keep bacon from curling in the pan?

Take away their little brooms.

Skating coach: *Did anyone laugh when you fell down?*
Skater: *No, but the ice made some awful cracks.*

What is the messiest sport
played in Canada?

Basketball, because the players
dribble on the floor.

Why did the Canada goose run
onto the soccer field?

Because the referee called a foul.

What sport do circles like to play?

Ring*ette.*

Why did the paddle get a cellphone?

It loved kayaking all the time.

What is the hardest
part about skating?

*The ice — when you
get right down to it!*

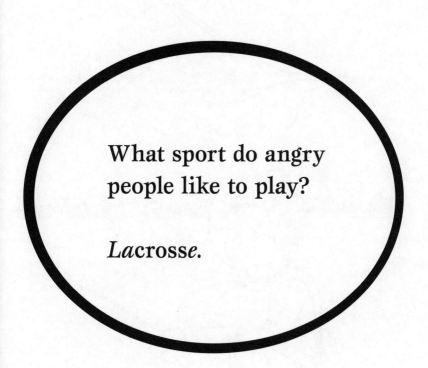

What sport do angry
people like to play?

Lacrosse.

196

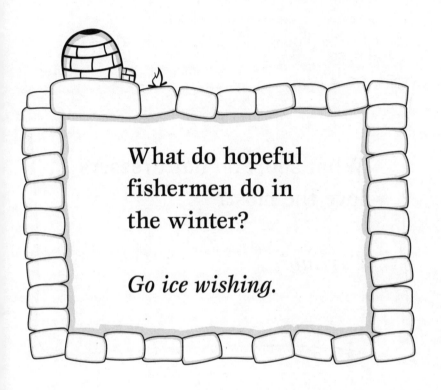

What do hopeful
fishermen do in
the winter?

Go ice wishing.

What sport do hairdressers love the most?

Curling!

What did the rapper
sing at the beginning
of the baseball game?

"Yo Canada."

201

Which team won the toboggan race?

The skeleton crew.

Where do monsters go swimming?

At the wreck centre.

What was the poltergeist's favourite track and field event?

Shock put.

What is Frankenstein's favourite track and field event?

The 100-metre smash.

Why are werewolves unpopular referees?

Because they're always calling howls.

What did Frankenstein do when the official fired the starter pistol?

He bolted.

Which creeps won the monsters' bonspiel?

The witches; no one is better with brooms.

What's a favourite winter sport
at the graveyard?

The skeleton race.

Why did the banshee join the
volleyball team?

She was a scream player.

What is a witch's favourite sport?

Cackle football.

Why do wraiths make good cheerleaders?

Because they're all spirit.

Why did the hockey player take up fishing?

He was good at hooking!

What did the hockey player use as a paddle?

A Bobby Orr!

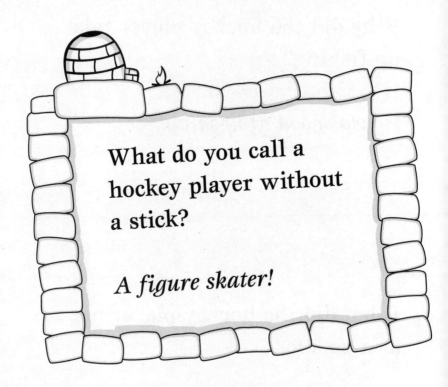

What do you call a hockey player without a stick?

A figure skater!

CREEPY

CANADA

Where do zombie farmers store their crops?

In brain elevators.

How do skeletons like their roast beef?

With gravey and hearse radish.

What do orphan monsters eat at the foundling school?

Ghoul gruel.

Why was the ogress having nightmares?

It might have been someone she ate.

215

What do health-conscious zombies eat for breakfast?

Whole-brain cereal.

Why did the zombie put his lunch in the ice box?

He wanted a brain freeze.

What's a banshee's favourite drink?

Scream soda.

What did the swamp monsters
serve the wizard for dinner?

Wormicelli in presto sauce.

What's a ghost's favourite food?

Ghoulash.

What do zombies order at the ice cream shop?

Hand shakes.

What does a ghost eat for breakfast?

Scream of wheat with fresh booberries.

Why were vampires the worst prospectors?

Because they wooden stake a claim.

Where do teenage werewolves hang out?

At the shopping maul.

What's the most popular Internet search engine?

Ghoulgle.

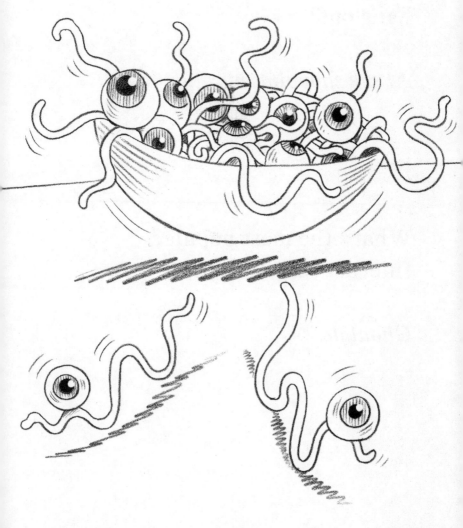

What do ghosts have for dinner?

Spookghetti and eyeballs.

Why do ghosts need security guards at their parties?

Because everyone's dying to get in.

Where can ghosts look up popular video clips?

On BooTube.

Why is the invisible man such a
bad liar?

*Because everyone can see right
through him.*

Why was Dr. Frankenstein such
a great comedian?

*Because he always left the
audience in stitches.*

What did the zombie give
his sweetheart?

A bouquet of noses.

230

Why did the vampire go to the dentist?

To improve his bite.

Who helped Bigfoot get to the ball?

Her hairy godmother.

What is a siren's favourite jewellery?

Fearings.

What's a vampire's favourite holiday?

Fangsgiving.

Why do vampires make good proofreaders?

Because they can always spot the Type Os.

Why did the ghost get a ticket?

For haunting without a licence.

Why doesn't a ghost scream
when it stubs its toe?

Because big ghouls don't cry.

Why did the witch love staying
at the hotel?

Because of the great broom service.

Funny Faceoffs

What is a hockey player's least favourite part of an airplane ride?

Boarding!

What kind of hats do hockey players hate to wear?

Salary caps!

Why did the new goalie bring a pen to practice?

He was told he'd be given hockey pads!

What do you call a hockey
player who writes scripts?

*A play*maker!

How did the hockey player pay
for his cool new clothes?

With a hip cheque!

Why did the hockey player get a promotion at work?

Because she worked overtime!

What do you call a hockey player who loves fruit?

A cherry picker!

Why were the team's gloves too big?

They were short-handed!

What do you call a group of players that keeps gaining weight?

An expansion team!

How do goalies hunt?

With a net!

Why did the hockey player
believe in aliens?

He kept seeing saucer passes!

How do you know which hockey
players dye their hair?

They're on the highlight reel!

How does a hockey player know when a girl likes him?

He gets called up!

What do you call a hockey player who borrows his equipment?

A rental player!

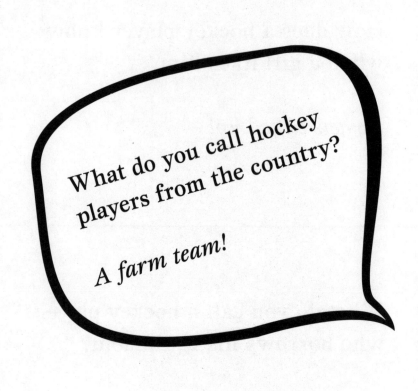

247

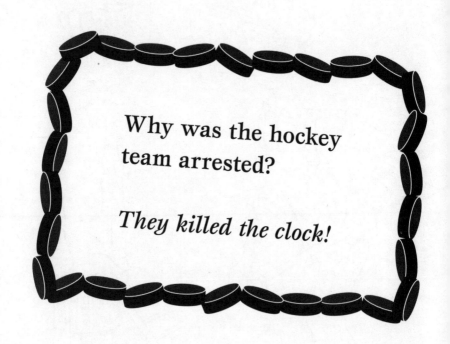

Why was the hockey
team arrested?

They killed the clock!

Why are hockey players so messy?

Because they have scrumbs everywhere!

Why do hockey players like giving autographs?

Because they get signing bonuses!

Why do hockey players pick up
sewing so easily?

*They already know how to thread
the needle!*

What did the girl hockey stick
say to the boy hockey stick?

Puck*er up!*

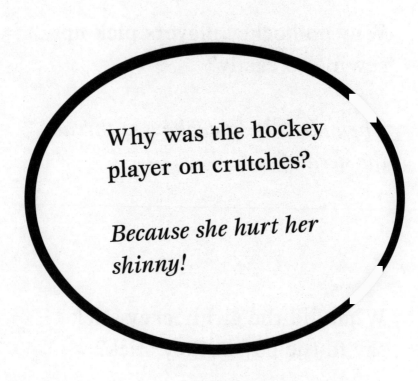

Why was the hockey player on crutches?

Because she hurt her shinny!

253

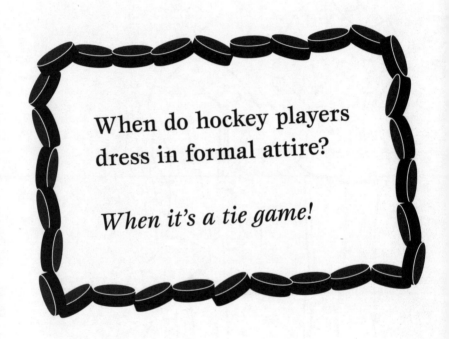

When do hockey players dress in formal attire?

When it's a tie game!

What did the coach say after
he took his defencemen out for
dinner?

Check please!

What do you call a hockey
player who drives a boat?

The captain!

Why did the hockey puck quit
the team?

It was tired of being slapped!

Why was the hockey player so
quick to stand up for himself?

He was a defenceman!

Where do coaches get sent when they misbehave?

To the Coach's Corner!

Why can't knights play hockey?

They keep getting penalties for spearing.

What do the coach's home renovations and team practices have in common?

They both have lots of drills!

Why is it always so cold in hockey arenas?

Because there are lots of fans!

What do you call it when hockey players try to get dates on the ice?

Pickup hockey!

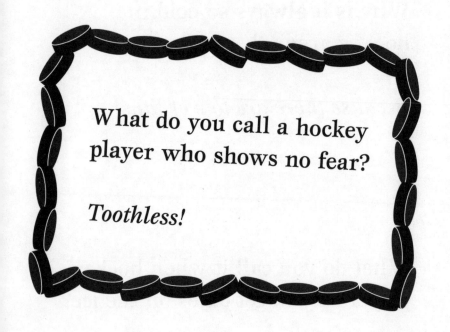

What do you call a hockey player who shows no fear?

Toothless!

Why did the hockey player call 911 when his shot was blocked?

Because he was robbed!

What do an outdoor ice rink and a rookie have in common?

They can both crack under pressure!

Where do you send someone who doesn't like hockey?

To the Hall of Lame!

Who is the prickliest hockey player in the league?

The one with the most points!

What do you call a hockey player after he escapes jail?

A breakout player!

Why did the hockey player go to the doctor?

For a check*up!*

What do you call a hockey player who watches what he says?

A mouth guard!

Why do athletes love to play hockey in Canada?

Because it's cooler here!

What is Wayne Gretzky's favourite bakery?

The Great Bun!

What's it called when a player is kicked out of a game for not wearing pants?

Unshortsmanlike conduct!

When do hockey players send most of their mail?

In the post season!

Teacher: *Give me a sentence using the word "indisposition."*
Pupil: *I always play centre in hockey because I love playing in-dis-position.*

Why did the hockey player ace the math test?

Because he cross-checked his answers.

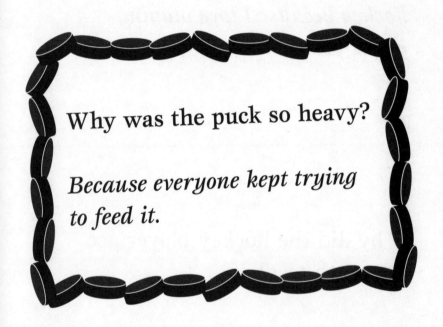

Why was the puck so heavy?

Because everyone kept trying to feed it.

What do you call a hockey player in outer space?

An all-star!

Time for School

How do you spell Canada?

C, eh? N, eh? D, eh?

Teacher: *How did the Vikings send secret messages?*
Student: *By Norse code.*

Mother: *Why aren't you doing very well in Canadian history?*
Kid: *Because the teacher keeps asking about things that happened before I was born!*

Teacher: *Why did the voyageurs cross the country in canoes?*
Student: *Because they didn't want to wait 150 years for a train.*

Teacher: *Where was the British North America Act signed?*
Student: *At the bottom.*

Teacher: *Name the first settler in the West.*
Student: *The Sun!*

What's the smartest province?

Newfoundland and Labrador, because it has four As and a B!

Teacher: *How do you spell Saskatchewan?*
Student: *The province or the river?*

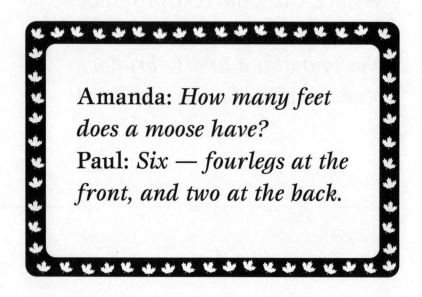

Amanda: *How many feet does a moose have?*
Paul: *Six — fourlegs at the front, and two at the back.*

Student: *My teacher was mad at me because I don't know where the Rockies are.*
Mother: *Well, next time remember where you put things!*

Teacher: *Who succeeded Canada's first prime minister?*
Student: *The second one!*

Where did the mad scientist get his degree?

At booniversity.

Why are Canadian students so smart?

They get a lot of ehs.

Teacher: Why do birds fly south for the winter? Student: Because it's too far to walk.

What do you get when you cross a beaver and a student?

Something that goes through pencils like crazy!

What do banshees learn
in language class?

The parts of screech.

Why did the monster raise her hand in class?

She had to go to the little ghoul's room.

Who was the teacher's favourite hockey player?

The one who kept passing!

What do circles eat at
Thanksgiving?

Pumpkin pi!

What kind of triangle loves
to skate?

An iceosceles triangle!

What do swamp monsters learn in math class?

Their slimes tables.

Why did the hockey player get kicked out of art class?

She drew a penalty!

Why was the math teacher such a good cowboy?

He was used to rounding up numbers.

Guess My Name

1. I have feet and legs but nothing else.
2. Use me well and I am everybody. Scratch my back and I am nobody.
3. I float on the water as light as a feather, yet a thousand men can't lift me.
4. You and everybody else have seen me, but you can never see me again.
5. I go up and down, twist round and round, but never ever move.
6. I live in winter, die in summer, and grow with my roots upwards.

7. If you feed me I will live, but if you give me water I die.

8. I am neither in the house nor out of the house, but I still am part of the house.

9. I run all the way from Toronto to Vancouver, but never move.

10. I am nothing but holes tied to holes, yet I am as strong as steel.

11. If my name is spoken, I am broken.

12. I am too much for one, just right for two, but nothing at all for three.

13. I am filled every morning and emptied every night, except once a year when I am filled at night and emptied in the morning.

14. I have a bank but no money; I have branches but no leaves.

15. I stand on one foot and have my heart in my head.

Answers on page 380.

ANIMAL COUNTRY

What do you get when you cross a pig with a killer whale?

A porca.

What do you get when you cross
a walrus with a shopaholic?

A mallrus!

What did the elk say to the
caribou when it fell through
the ice?

Oh deer!

What do you get when you cross a polar bear and a cougar?

I don't know, but you'd better run quick.

What do Canadian horses say?

N-eh?

What do Canadian cows say?

Moo, silly!

What did the patriotic snail sing?

"Slow Canada."

What do you get when you cross
a vampire with a beaver?

I don't know, but I bet it has an
awful bite.

How do you know caribou are scared of ghosts?

You can see their moosebumps.

What's red and white with
a wicked bite?

Santa Jaws.

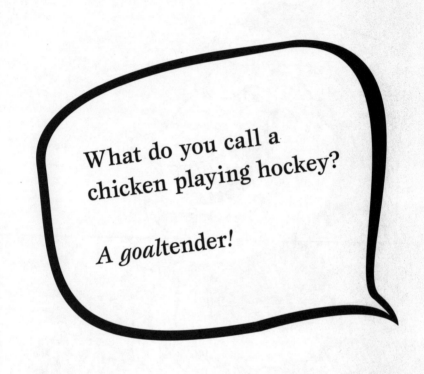

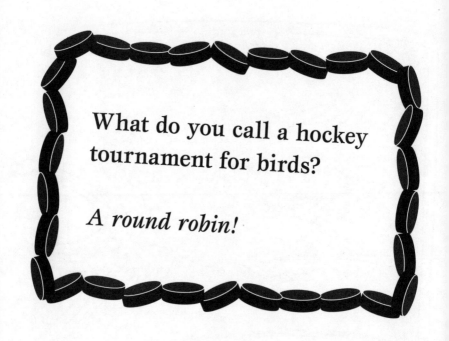

What do you call a hockey
tournament for birds?

A round robin!

What do you get when you hire a pig at an arena?

A Hamboni driver!

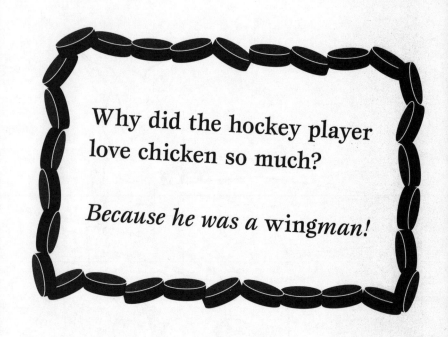

Why did the hockey player love chicken so much?

Because he was a wingman!

321

What does a bird do before he gives up the puck?

Feathers the pass!

Why did the pig have to sit out the game?

He'd pulled a hamstring!

Why did the otter cross the road?

To get to the otter side.

Why did the duck cross the road?

Because the chicken retired and moved to Florida.

Why did the buffalo cross the road?

It was the chicken's day off.

Why did the lobster cross the road?

To get to the other tide.

What did the sporty chicken do?

He lacrossed the road.

Why did the chicken cross the road?

Because the zombie was chasing it.

Why did the Albertosaurus cross the road?

To escape from the terrordactyl.

Why didn't the ghost hunter cross the road?

Because he wasn't a chicken.

Why has no one ever spotted a leopard in Canada?

Because leopards already have spots!

What Really Bugs Us

What is a mosquito's favourite sport?

Skin-diving.

How do you know if you have a tough mosquito?

You slap him and he slaps you back.

What has six legs, bites and talks in code?

A morsequito.

Why did the mosquito go to the dentist?

To get his bite checked.

What has antlers and sucks blood?

A moosequito.

What insects love math class?

Mosquitoes — they add to misery, subtract from pleasure, divide your attention and multiply quickly.

What kind of bug repellant does a light bulb wear?

OFF!

What did the doctor say to the new mosquito mother?

There's a sucker born every minute!

What do you call a hockey
player who swats bees?

A buzzer beater!

What do you get when you cross
a computer and one million
mosquitoes?

A gigabite.

How do insects get around in the winter?

On Bee-Doos.

Why are there no
vampires in Manitoba?

*They can't compete
with the mosquitoes.*

339

Home Ice Advantage

Why do Toronto's players always think they're going to win the Stanley Cup?

Because they beLeaf in themselves!

How do the Canadiens get to
the Bell Centre?

They take Hab rides!

What kind of art does Edmonton
have in its locker room?

Oiler paintings.

Why did the boy climb up a tree with his hockey stick?

Because he wanted to play with the Maple Leafs.

343

Which team has the strongest swimmers?

The San Jose Sharks!

Where can you find flames on ice?

At the Calgary Saddledome!

Which team is the goofiest?

The Vancouver Canuckleheads.

Why did the Ducks miss the season opener?

They had to fly south for the winter.

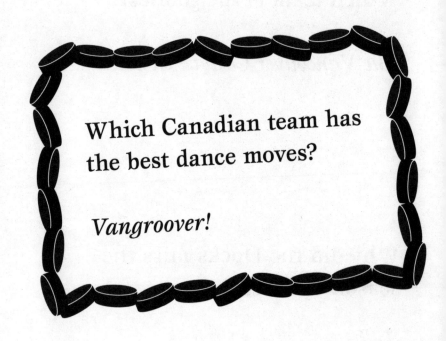

Which Canadian team has the best dance moves?

Vangroover!

Which team waddles onto the ice?

The Pittsburgh Penguins!

Which team likes to wreck everything?

The Edmonton Spoilers.

Which team has to avoid firefighters?

The Calgary Flames.

What do you get if you cross New Jersey's team with a chicken?

Devilled eggs.

Which team prints everything
in big letters?

The Washington CAPITALS.

What do you get when you cross
a Canadien with a newspaper?

*Something that is blue, white and
red all over.*

How did the Sharks fix their broken bench?

With a hammerhead.

Who beat the Woolly Mammoths in the Ice Age playoffs?

The Buffalo Sabertooths.

Snow Much Fun

What do snowmen wear on their heads?

Ice caps.

Where do snowmen go to dance?

*Snow*balls.

What happened when the snowgirl broke up with the snowboy?

She gave him the cold shoulder.

How do snowmen make their beds?

With sheets of ice and blankets of snow.

How do snowmen travel around?

By icicle.

What two letters of the alphabet
do snowmen prefer?

I.C.

What do you get if you cross a
snowman and a shark?

Frost bite.

What do snowmen eat
for lunch?

Icebergers.

Where do snowmen keep their money?

In a snow bank.

What is plowed but never planted?

Snow.

Curtis: *Great news, the teacher says we have a test today come rain or shine.*
Paul: *So what's so great about that?*
Curtis: *It's snowing!*

What happened when the icicle landed on the girl's head?

It knocked her cold!

When is a canoe like a heap of snow?

When it's adrift.

What did the man put on his car when the weather was cold?

An extra muffler.

How many seasons does Canada have?

Two — six months of winter and six months of poor snowmobiling.

What would you do if the country was flooded?

Drink Canada Dry!

Why do skeletons hate winter?

Because the wind goes right through them.

How do you make antifreeze?

Take away her housecoat.

Why is snow easier to understand than any other weather?

Because you can catch the drift.

Where do arctic hamburgers come from?

The bundra.

How does Bigfoot tell time?

With a saskwatch!

What does the abominable snowman do when he's scared of the dark?

He cuddles with a blanket of snow.

How do ghosts travel in the winter?

By Ski-Boos.

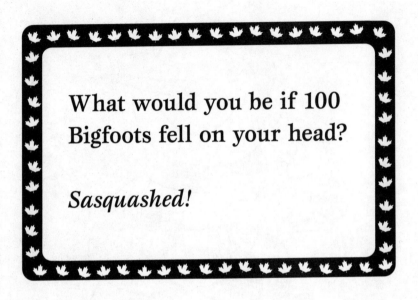

What would you be if 100 Bigfoots fell on your head?

Sasquashed!

What do snowmen
play with?

Teddy brrrrrs.

Why did the abominable
snowman attack the glacier?

*Because it wanted to make
ice scream.*

Why do ghouls gather on the
winter solstice?

*To celebrate the longest fright of
the year.*

Why don't goalies get sunburned at the beach?

They wear blockers!

What did the hockey player do when the weather got warmer?

He dropped his gloves!

Why did the Zamboni driver call a plumber?

Because the ice was flooded!

What do snowmen eat for
breakfast?

Frosted Flakes.

What did the sea say to the
iceberg?

Nothing. It just waved.

Where does Santa stay when he isn't at the North Pole?

In a ho-ho-hotel.

If a farmer raises wheat in dry weather, what does he raise in wet weather?

An umbrella.

Answers:

Riddle, Riddle!, page 31
1. when it runs; 2. when they're in quarters; 3. the crane;
4. when it rains (reigns); 5. the buttercup; 6. noise; 7. it has
two banks; 8. because they can't walk in it

Canadian Riddles, page 163
1. because he's alive; 2. the buck and the doe (get it, dough?);
3. halfway — after that, he's running out; 4. no! He's dead;
5. white — the house is at the North Pole

Guess My Name, pages 300–301
1. stockings; 2. a mirror; 3. bubble; 4. yesterday; 5. a road;
6. icicle; 7. fire; 8. a window; 9. a railroad track; 10. a chain;
11. silence; 12. a secret; 13. a stocking; 14. a river; 15. a cabbage